WILDLIFE ODDITIES

MYSTIFYING MAMMALS

MASON CREST

MASON CREST

450 Parkway Drive, Suite D
Broomall, PA 19008
(866) MCP-BOOK (toll free)
www.masoncrest.com

Developed and produced by Mason Crest

First printing

9 8 7 6 5 4 3 2 1

ISBN (hardback) 978-1-4222-3525-6
ISBN (series) 978-1-4222-3523-2
ISBN (ebook) 978-1-4222-8345-5

Cataloging-in-Publication Data on file with the Library of Congres

WILDLIFE ODDITIES

INCREDIBLE INSECTS

MYSTIFYING MAMMALS

PECULIAR PLANTS

REMARKABLE REPTILES

SHOCKING SEA CREATURES

PICTURE CREDITS

CONTENTS

KEY ICONS TO LOOK FOR:

Words to Understand: These words with their easy-to-understand definitions will increase the reader's understanding of the text while building vocabulary skills.

Sidebars: This boxed material within the main text allows readers to build knowledge, gain insights, explore possibilities, and broaden their perspectives by weaving together additional information to provide realistic and holistic perspectives.

Text-Dependent Questions: These questions send the reader back to the text for more careful attention to the evidence presented there.

Research Projects: Readers are pointed toward areas of further inquiry connected to each chapter. Suggestions are provided for projects that encourage deeper research and analysis.

ONE BIG FAMILY

Mammals take many different shapes. People are mammals—as are whales, elephants, and mice. Though we are all very different, there are a few traits we all have in common (like hair). And together, we make up of one of the main groups of animals on Earth today.

⬆ *Some mammals, such as this beluga whale, spend their whole lives in water.*

The mammal group includes many weird and wonderful creatures. Scaly armadillos, spiky porcupines, long-nosed tapirs, and night-loving bats are all part of this family of animals. There are about 4,000 different kinds of mammals.

Mammals vary a lot in size. Blue whales are the largest mammals. It weighs 25 times as much as the largest land mammal, the African elephant. The hefty elephant weighs as much as 100 adult people. The world's smallest mammal is Kitti's hog-nosed bat, which is the size of a bumblebee!

SIDEBAR

MAMMAL BABIES NEED THEIR MAMAS

Most mammal mothers give birth to fully formed babies rather than laying eggs like birds and reptiles. These babies, though, are not ready to live on their own. Babies feed on their mother's milk. Adult mammals look after their young and may teach them the skills they need in life.

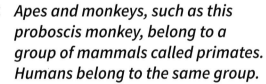

Apes and monkeys, such as this proboscis monkey, belong to a group of mammals called primates. Humans belong to the same group.

Many mammal babies stay with their parents for months or even years. When piglets are suckling, a sow can produce two and a half gallons a day.

GLOBE-TROTTERS

Go for a swim, and you'll find a mammal. Just look up, and you could find a mammal. Push over a rock, and there might be a mammal there, too. Mammals can be found all over the world. Bats fly through the air, and monkeys swing through the treetops. Moles live underground.

On land, mammals are found in tropical jungles, pine forests, grasslands, and even high in the mountains. Sheep, cows, and horses are domesticated mammals that live and work with humans. Dogs and cats share our homes as pets. But most mammals run wild!

NIGHTTIME NEIGHBORS   Mammals such as foxes, raccoons, and rats make their homes in crowded cities. They mostly hide by day and come out to look for food at night. When we are asleep, they search through our garbage to find food scraps.

Mammals are warm-blooded. Amazingly, their body temperature stays about the same even when it is very cold or hot. This means that mammals can survive in harsh places such as icy Arctic wastes and hot, dry deserts. However, keeping an even body temperature uses up lots of energy, so mammals need to eat a lot of food.

▲ *The strange-looking mole makes its home in an underground burrow. A strong swimmer, it finds its food in ponds and streams.*

◄◄

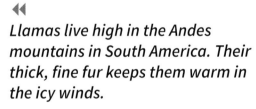

Llamas live high in the Andes mountains in South America. Their thick, fine fur keeps them warm in the icy winds.

◄◄

Elephant seals spend most of their lives in the oceans but come ashore to breed on rocky beaches. Only the males have swollen snouts that look like elephants' trunks.

USE IT OR LOSE IT

All mammals have a bony skeleton, though those bones can come in very different shapes and sizes. The bones we use in our hands to write are the same bones that help bats fly. All mammals also have hair covering their bodies, though some have more than others. (Baby dolphins are born with a mustache!)

Mammals have similar bodies, however large or small they are. Land mammals all have four limbs, and most have a tail, though humans don't. Dolphins and whales look a lot like fish, but they are also mammals. Their front limbs have developed into flippers, and their back legs have disappeared altogether. Their smooth, tapering shape helps them swim through the water easily.

🔺 *The kinkajou uses its tail as an extra limb to hang onto branches. Other mammals use their tails to flick away flies or to balance when running along tree branches.*

 SIDEBAR

A LONG WINTER'S NAP Some mammals survive the winter cold by falling into an amazing deep sleep called hibernation. They hardly breathe, and their heart beats very slowly. They use little energy. Groundhogs retreat to their burrows to hibernate in autumn. Strangely, all groundhogs wake up on about the same day in spring, usually at the start of February.

All mammals groom or clean their fur to keep it in good condition. Macaque monkeys help one another by removing ticks and fleas.

The hair on mammals' bodies helps them to keep warm. In cold weather, the hairs stand up to trap a layer of warm air next to the skin. Musk oxen of the Arctic have the longest hair of any mammal, except for humans. Mammals that live in cold water, such as seals and whales, have an extra layer of fat, called blubber, under their skin. This keeps them warm even though they have close to no hair.

Manatees are water-dwelling mammals, like seals, whales, and dolphins. They swim along by beating their powerful tails up and down.

MAMMALS LIKE TO MOVE IT

When you want to move, you have many choices. Do you like to jump, skip, or roll? All mammals like to move in their own special ways. Some creep along quite slowly. Others swim, fly, hop, or run at great speed.

In the African grasslands, cheetahs race along at up to 70 miles per hour (95 km/h). Kangaroos are the fastest mammals on two legs—and they are champion hoppers. Killer whales are the fastest mammals in the oceans, swimming up to 34 miles per hour (55 km/h).

Verreaux's sifaka, a type of lemur, is equally agile in the trees and on the ground.

SIDEBAR

SWEET FEET
Mammals have differently shaped feet that help them to move about in their surroundings. Elephants have pillar-like legs and feet to support their great weight. A sloth's curved claws are ideal for hooking around branches. Moles have front feet shaped like shovels that help them burrow through soil.

In the tropical forests of South America, sloths spend long hours sleeping. They move very little. Tiny plants called algae grow in their fur and give it a greenish color. ▶▶

Flying squirrels cannot really fly, but they have furry flaps of skin between their front and hind legs that they use for gliding. The outstretched skin acts as a parachute, allowing the squirrel to swoop from tree to tree. ◀◀

Bats are the only mammals that can truly fly. They glide through the air on skin-covered wings, looking for insects or sweet nectar to eat. Bats are nocturnal—they are awake at night. They spend the daylight hours hanging upside down asleep.

THE BETTER TO SEE YOU WITH

Like people, mammals use five main senses to interact with their world—sight, hearing, smell, taste, and touch.   Most use one sense more than the others. And some have special sixth senses that don't fit into these categories.

Humans mostly use sight. Dogs, foxes, and wolves rely on their keen senses of hearing and smell instead. A bloodhound can track someone just by following the smell of their footprints.

SIDEBAR

EAR PROTECTION
Many mammals have keen hearing to alert them to the danger of predators. Jackrabbits listen for enemies with their large ears, which turn around to pinpoint sounds. Mammals are the only animals to have ears on the outsides of their heads. In hot places, jackrabbits lose a lot of heat through their ears. This helps them to keep cool.

A little brown fruit bat swoops among the branches, guided by its super sense of echolocation.

Sight is a lot less important to other mammals who hunt in darkness or in murky water. Bushbabies are small, monkey-like creatures. They live in the forests of Africa. Their huge eyes and large, sensitive ears help them to catch flying insects even in dim light.

Bats and dolphins use an amazing super sense called echolocation to catch their prey. They make high-pitched sounds when they are hunting. These sounds bounce off animals close by, and the bat or dolphin can hear the returning echo. This helps them to find their prey. Echolocation also helps bats to move around easily in the dark.

In Australia, duck-billed platypuses hunt in muddy streams and rivers. They search for worms, fish, and insects with their extraordinary touch-sensitive bills (beaks).

Like apes, monkeys, and humans, bushbabies see in color. Most other mammals probably see in black and white.

The duck-billed platypus uses its amazing beak to sense tiny electrical charges given off by swimming creatures. This mammal looks so weird that when the first specimens were brought to Europe, experts thought they were fakes.

DINNER TIME!

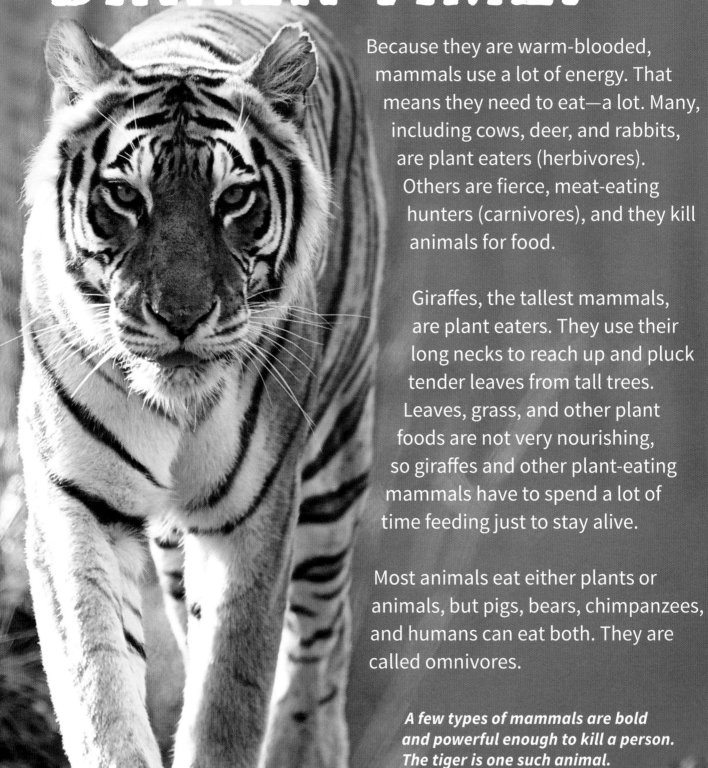

Because they are warm-blooded, mammals use a lot of energy. That means they need to eat—a lot. Many, including cows, deer, and rabbits, are plant eaters (herbivores). Others are fierce, meat-eating hunters (carnivores), and they kill animals for food.

Giraffes, the tallest mammals, are plant eaters. They use their long necks to reach up and pluck tender leaves from tall trees. Leaves, grass, and other plant foods are not very nourishing, so giraffes and other plant-eating mammals have to spend a lot of time feeding just to stay alive.

Most animals eat either plants or animals, but pigs, bears, chimpanzees, and humans can eat both. They are called omnivores.

A few types of mammals are bold and powerful enough to kill a person. The tiger is one such animal.

Many meat-eating mammals have special colors and markings on their fur that help them hide in their natural surroundings. This is called camouflage, or disguise, and means the hunting animal can creep up on its prey without being seen. In a zoo, a tiger's black-and-orange coat may stand out and look obvious, but the same stripes conceal the big cat in its jungle home.

Giraffes are extraordinary creatures with incredibly long necks, slender legs, and mottled coloring. The first Europeans to see them in Africa could hardly believe their eyes.

▶▶

◀◀

The aye-aye is a strange lemur from the woods of Madagascar. It has an extra-long, thin middle finger that it uses to hook out juicy insects from under tree bark.

SIDEBAR

WHAT'S ON THE MENU?
All kinds of creatures are hunted by mammals. Big cats such as lions and tigers prey on other mammals and also birds. Shrews and hedgehogs eat worms and insects. Marsh mongooses hunt crabs, fish, frogs, and snakes.

SURVIVAL IS NO GAME FOR MAMMALS

Being a mammal in the wild is no picnic. In fact, if they're not careful, they could be part of another animal's picnic! Mammals use many different tools to stay alert and escape possible attackers. Some swim, hop, or run away as quickly as possible. Others have secret weapons or tricks to keep off the menu.

Many mammals use camouflage to help them blend in with their surroundings and hide from danger. A zebra's stripes hide it among the grasses of the African plains and may even help them keep cool. A deer's spotted coat helps conceal it in shady woods.

◀◀
The porcupine's prickly spines protect it from predators.

THE EYES HAVE IT

The position of a mammal's eyes can tell you if it is a creature that hunts or one that is hunted. Deer and rabbits, for example, have eyes set on the sides of their heads, so they can spot danger from all around. Predators such as cats have eyes that look forward, so they can focus and pounce on their prey.

Some mammals have natural armor that protects them when they are threatened. Porcupines and hedgehogs are covered with sharp spines. When cornered, a hedgehog rolls itself into a spiny ball. The porcupine turns the sharp spikes on its back toward its enemy—the spikes come off easily and stick in the predator's mouth.

▶▶

The Virginia opossum has a clever trick to get out of trouble. If a predator spots it, it drops to the ground and lies still, playing dead. Most predators will not touch dead animals, so they move on.

◀◀

The armadillo is built like a tank, with a covering of tough, bony plates all over its upper body. When threatened, it rolls into a ball to protect its soft belly.

ALL IN THE FAMILY

Mammals, like other animals, spend part of their adult lives having and raising young—with some (the naked mole rat) up to 30 at a time! Most baby mammals develop inside their mother's body, and when they come out, their mothers take care of them. But there are a few strange exceptions to this rule.

In the breeding season, male and female mammals meet up to mate. Many males establish special areas called territories, where they show off to the opposite sex. Some males get into terrible battles with their rivals to find out who is strongest. Only the winners get the chance to mate.

▲ *This female tenrec has an unusually large litter (group of babies). She can rear up to 24 young successfully.*

 SIDEBAR

BEFORE BIRTH Baby mammals spend different amounts of time in the womb before they are ready to be born. This time is called gestation. Mice take less than three weeks to grow. Humans take nine months. Asian elephants take more than 20 months, the longest time of all.

Most baby mammals develop inside their mother's womb, where they are fed by an organ called the placenta. They are born fully formed. The group of marsupials, which includes kangaroos, develops in a different way. The baby kangaroo is born early, when it is still tiny and unfinished. It crawls up into the warm pouch on its mother's belly, where it finishes growing.

A third, small group of mammals called monotremes have even more unusual breeding habits. They lay eggs instead of giving birth to live babies as other mammals do. Of 4,000 different mammals, only three are monotremes: the platypus and two species of echidna.

Male hippos fight for the right to mate and lead the herd of females. Rivals open their jaws wide to frighten one another. Then they lunge forward and attack their opponent with their teeth.

⩔

▲ *The female echidna lays a single, leathery egg, which develops inside a skin pouch on her belly. The baby hatches after about 10 days.*

19.

POSITIVE PARENTING

Most animals are on their own right when they're born. The mother just lays her eggs and leaves. Luckily for us humans, mammals have a different approach. They stick around and care for their babies. Many spend weeks or even years not only feeding their young but teaching them how to survive.

Mammals are the only animals that produce food for their babies from their own bodies. All baby mammals feed on their mother's milk. The milk contains all the nourishment that the baby needs.

This baby kangaroo, or joey, is finishing its development in its mother's pouch.

◄◄

Mouse opossums are South American marsupials. Females give birth to about 10 tiny, helpless babies. They complete their development in their mother's pouch and later ride around on her back.

At birth, some mammal babies, such as mice, are bald, blind, and helpless. Others, including newborn lambs and calves, are furry and can stand and walk right away.

Baby mammals are born knowing how to do certain things, such as drink their mother's milk. Other skills have to be learned. The young learn hunting and survival skills by watching their parents and through practice. Playing with brothers and sisters also helps to strengthen muscles and develop hunting skills.

These young red fox cubs are play fighting. This helps them to grow stronger and teaches them hunting skills.

SIDEBAR

GROWING UP FAST   Small mammals such as mice produce many babies that grow up very quickly. In just a few weeks, the young are fully grown and able to produce babies themselves. Larger mammals have fewer babies that grow up much more slowly. Human children take the longest time of all to grow up, perhaps because we have so much to learn.

WHAT MAKES A FAMILY?

When we think of family, we think of moms, dads, sister, brothers, aunts, uncles, cousins, and grandparents. Many wild mammals live alone except when the females are raising babies. Others spend most or all their lives in a group. Some even mate for life, like Lar gibbons, Malagasy giant rats, and prairie voles.

Group life provides safety for all kinds of mammals, especially those that are hunted by predators. On the grasslands of Africa, zebras and antelopes live in big herds. While the herd is grazing, each animal looks up from time to time to check for danger. It warns the others if it sees a threat approaching. Then the whole herd gallops off.

Young elephants grow up in a herd. There are about 10 closely related females and their babies. Aunts and grown-up cousins help with baby care. Females stay with the herd when they grow up. Males leave to join a small group of males or live on their own. ▼

▸▸ *Dolphins live and hunt in a group called a school. They whistle to one another to organize their movements as they spread out to surround a shoal of fish.*

◂◂ *Meerkats live in large, underground colonies. To watch for danger, they rear right up on their back legs.*

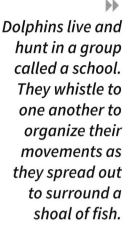

SIDEBAR

GROUPTHINK

Mammal groups have different names. A group of lions is called a pride. Killer whales hunt in a pod, dolphins in a school. Monkeys live in troupes, and bats roost in colonies. Can you find out any other mammal group names?

Among lions, wolves, and dolphins, the group is also a hunting party. Group members work together to hunt faster or larger prey than they could on their own. It is mainly female lions who do the hunting. African hunting dogs band together to tackle prey as large as zebras and wildebeest.

ON THEIR LAST LEGS?

Wild mammals are no strangers to danger. On any given day, they have to face storms, droughts, sickness, or predators. Nowadays, however, the biggest danger comes from human beings. Climate change and loss of habitat mean some of the weirdest, wildest mammals are in danger of dying out altogether.

For centuries, people have hunted mammals such as whales, deer, and buffalo for meat. Cheetahs and other big cats have been shot for their beautiful skins. Wild mammals such as rhinos and tigers have been killed because people think they are dangerous or that their body parts have healing powers. Now many of these amazing creatures are very rare.

A mountain gorilla rests in the grass in a forest in West Africa. Mountain gorillas are in danger of dying out because they are hunted by people.

THERE'S NO PLACE LIKE HOME

Humans often destroy the homes of other mammals when they clear forests and grasslands to build new towns and roads. As more and more natural places are destroyed, there is less and less space for wild mammals to live safely. This is called habitat destruction.

Nowadays, more people are starting to care that beautiful mammals such as pandas and gorillas may die out altogether. All over the world, parks and reserves have been set up to help them survive. Some rare mammals have been bred in zoos and then released into the wild. You can help by sponsoring a rare mammal or joining a conservation group (see page 31).

Giant pandas live in remote mountain forests in China. They are now very scarce in the wild.
▸▸

MYSTIFYING MAMMAL FACTS

The blue whale
This giant whale is the world's largest mammal. A big blue whale weighs 165 tons (150,000 kg) and may be 96 feet (32 m) long. Female whales grow bigger than the males.

Elephants
These are the largest land mammals, standing up to 11 feet (3.5 m) high and weighing up to 7 tons (6,350 kg). The rhinoceros is the second-largest mammal found on land.

Giraffes
These long-necked animals are the world's tallest mammals, towering up to 17.5 feet (5.8 m). They strip the tender leaves from the acacias and scrub growing in Africa.

Kitti's hog-nosed bat
This bat comes from Thailand and is the world's smallest mammal. It is a tiny creature weighing just 0.07 ounces (2 g), with a wingspan of 6 inches (15 cm). Its body is the size of a bumblebee.

Siberian tigers
These are the world's largest cats, measuring up to 10 feet (3.1 m) long from the nose to the tip of the tail. Unfortunately, these beautiful mammals are now very rare.

Giant primates
Gorillas are the largest primates—members of the ape and monkey group, which includes humans. A male lowland gorilla stands up to 6 feet (1.8 m) tall, shorter than the tallest human, but weighs up to 385 (175 kg).

◀◀
Walruses are the heaviest members of the seal family. Big males weigh up to 3,500 pounds (1,600 kg). Both sexes have long tusks.

South American capybara

This is the world's largest rodent (the mammal group that includes rats, mice, squirrels and voles). It grows up to 4 feet (1.4) m long. The northern pygmy mouse from North America is one of the smallest rodents.

Speedy cheetah

The cheetah is the fastest runner over a short distance, but it tires quite quickly. This large cat puts on a burst of speed to overtake prey.

The three-toed sloth

This odd creature comes from South America and is the world's slowest mammal. It spends four-fifths of its life sleeping.

Humans

Humans live longer than any other mammals, sometimes reaching ages of 105 or more.

Giant anteater

This creature has a very long tongue—up to 23 inches (60 cm) long. It uses it to slurp up ants and termites and eats up to 30,000 insects a day.

Sperm whales

These whales hold the record as the deepest divers among mammals. These large whales are thought to descend to depths of 9,000 feet (3,000 m) when hunting deep-sea prey.

Arctic ground squirrels

These animals spend longer in hibernation than any other mammal. In icy northern lands they spend up to 9 months asleep.

Mandrills are large, heavy monkeys from Africa. Only the male has bright colors on his nose and cheeks. ▼

MYSTIFYING MAMMAL WORDS

Blubber
A fatty layer found under the skin of mammals, such as seals and whales, that keeps them warm in cold water.

Camouflage
The colors and patterns on a mammal's fur, which help it to blend in with its surroundings, so it can hide from enemies or sneak up on prey.

Carnivore
An animal that eats mainly meat.

Habitat
The particular place where a mammal lives, such as a jungle or desert.

Hatch
When a fully developed baby animal breaks out of its shell.

Herbivore
An animal that eats plants.

Hibernation
A deep sleep that allows mammals to survive the winter cold.

Litter
A group of young all born to a female mammal at once.

Mammal
One of the group of animals that have a bony skeleton, have fur on their bodies, and feed their young on milk.

Marsupial
One of a group of mammals whose young are born at a very early stage and finish developing in the mother's pouch.

Hinge
A moveable joint in the skeleton, which means that a snake can stretch its jaws very wide.

Jacobson's organ
The sensitive area on the roof of a reptile's mouth that helps it to identify smells.

Keratin
The tough, horny material from which a reptile's scales are made. Your toenails and fingernails are made of the same material.

Mammal
One of a group of animals with fur on its body that feeds its babies on milk.

Monotreme
One of a small group of mammals that lay eggs instead of giving birth to live young.

Nocturnal
An animal that rests by day and is active at night.

Predator
An animal, such as a tiger or leopard, that catches and kills other animals for food.

Prey
An animal that is hunted for food, such as a rabbit that is hunted by eagles.

Primate
A member of the group of mammals that includes apes, monkeys, and humans.

Rodent
One of the large group of mammals that has chisel-shaped front teeth designed for gnawing plants.

Skeleton
The bony framework that supports the bodies of animals such as mammals and birds.

Species
A particular type of animal. The duck-billed platypus is a species of mammal. There are about 4,000 different species of mammals in all.

Sponsor
To pay for something, usually for a good cause. If you sponsor a rare mammal, you will be helping its species survive.

Warm-blooded
An animal whose body temperature stays about the same, whatever the temperature of its surroundings. Mammals and birds are warm-blooded animals.

TEXT-DEPENDENT QUESTIONS

1. How many different kinds of mammals are there?

2. What is the one thing that mammals do that no other animal group does?

3. What is alike in all mammal skeletons?

4. We all know about herbivores and carnivores, but what do omnivores eat?

5. Why is living in a herd a good thing?

▶▶

Tasmanian devils are marsupials from the island of Tasmania, south of Australia. They are mainly active at night

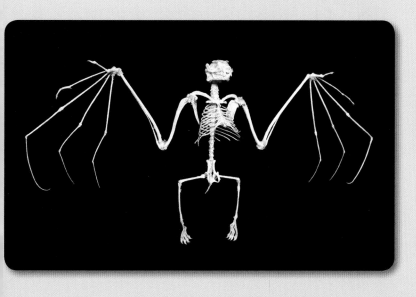

◀◀
Like all mammals, bats have a bony skeleton to support their bodies.

MYSTIFYING MAMMALS PROJECTS

MAKE A MAMMAL

There are some traits that make a mammal unique. Keeping this in mind, pretend you are a scientist who has discovered a new mammal species. Name your new mammal, and draw a picture of it. Then write a description of your animal, including what it looks like, where it lives, and what it eats. You can even include how the animal acts—if it lives in groups, how it acts toward people and other animals, and so on.

MAMMAL BOOK A–Z

There are more than 4,000 mammals. Can you find one that starts with A? How about B? Make a book where each page tells about a mammal starting with a letter of the alphabet. On each page, find or draw a picture of the animal. Be sure to include the animal's name. To make your book even more helpful to readers, you can list where the animal lives, what it eats, and any other details you can find.

SMELL LIKE A MAMMAL

Mammals like dogs and bears rely on their sense of smell to find food. Although much less sensitive, people use their sense of smell too. Now it's time to test how well you smell. Collect a set of glasses or jars, but it's important that you can't see through them. Decide what kinds of mammal food you'd like to put in your jars. Some suggestions are grass, honey, bananas, carrots, cookies, and so on. Place a tissue over the top of the jar, and secure it with a rubber band. Wait for a few minutes to let the smell build. Then it's time to test your friends! Have them take a sniff, and see if they can guess what's inside.

A mother tiger carries one of her cubs by holding it gently in her mouth.

MYSTIFYING MAMMALS ON THE WEB

Web of Life:
http://www.curator.org/weboflife

WWF Wildlife Conservation:
http://www.worldwildlife.org/initiatives/wildlife-conservation

Animal Planet:
http://www.animalplanet.com/wild-animals/mammals/

NeoK12
http://www.neok12.com/Mammals.htm

If you have access to the Internet, there are lots of Web sites where you can try to find out more about mammals. Web sites change from time to time, so don't worry if you can't find some of these sites. You can search for sites featuring your favorite mammals using any search engine. Include the mammal's scientific (Latin) name if you know it to narrow your search.

FURTHER READING

Alderton, David. *Mammals Around the World.* Mankato, MN: Smart Apple Media, 2015.

Boothroyd, Jennifer, *Endangered and Extinct Mammals.* Minneapolis, MN: Learner

Publications Company, 2014.

Costain, Meredith. *Mammals Great and Small.* New York: PowerKids Press, 2015.

Squire, Ann. *Mammals.* New York: Children's Press, 2014.

Thomas, Isabel. *Marvelous Mammals.* Chicago, IL: Raintree, 2013.

INDEX

In this index, bold italic font indicates a photo or illustration.